GILDED IMAGES

GILDED IMAGES
A Masquerade of Verse

Keith and Elizabeth Stanley-Mallett

ARTHUR H. STOCKWELL LTD
Torrs Park   Ilfracombe   Devon
Established 1898
www.ahstockwell.co.uk

© Keith & Elizabeth Stanley-Mallett, 2012
First published in Great Britain, 2012
All rights reserved.
No part of this publication may be reproduced
or transmitted in any form or by any means,
electronic or mechanical, including photocopy,
recording, or any information storage and
retrieval system, without permission
in writing from the copyright holder.

British Library Cataloguing-in-Publication Data.
A catalogue record for this book is available
from the British Library.

ISBN 978-0-7223-4204-6 Paperback edition.
ISBN 978-0-7223-4205-3 Cloth-bound edition.
Printed in Great Britain by
Arthur H. Stockwell Ltd
Torrs Park   Ilfracombe
Devon

Previously published poems by the same author:
  Little Traveller – Pumpkin Publications
  Conspiracy of Faculties – Poetry Now, Forward Press, 1994
  Yielding Forms – Poetry Now, 1994
  One, That are We – Poetry Now, 1994
  Two Minutes of Silence – Anchor Books, 1994
  A Norfolk Winter Sunset – Poets England Series, Brentham Press, 1994
  Come Silently to Me – Poetry Now, 1995
  To the Eye – Poetry Now, 1995
  World Wide Conceded Nationally – Poetry Now, 1996
  Three Times Twenty – Poetry Now, 1996
  I Believe in Betjeman – Poetry Now, 1996
  Emotive Machine – Poetry Now, 1996
  Essence of Time – Poetry Now, 1996
  Poetic Visions – Poetry Now, 1996
  Once Upon a Time – Poetry Now, 1996
  The Red Fox – Anchor Books, 1997
  Soul Winds – Poetry Now, 1997
  Across a Timeless Threshold – Anchor Books, 1999
  Mrs Batholomew's Door – Anchor Books, 1999
  Electronic Life – United Press, 1999
  Under An Indigo Moon – Arthur H. Stockwell Ltd, 2009
  Beneath Rose-Lemon Skies – Arthur H. Stockwell Ltd, 2009
  Before the Rainbow Fades – Arthur H. Stockwell Ltd, 2010
  Between Night and Dancing Light – Arthur H. Stockwell Ltd, 2010
  Beyond the Last Horizon – Arthur H. Stockwell Ltd, 2010
  Upon a Past and Future Path – Arthur H. Stockwell Ltd, 2011
  Odd Wit and Other Bits – Arthur H. Stockwell Ltd, 2011

FOREWORD

BOOK VIII

The first part of this book, Part I, is my eighth work of verse. Although not a part of my original series, it is, however, of a character that is justifiably fitting by its content, as a complementary work; and it differs marginally in style both in context and spirit. I hope readers will find this book of some interest.

Keith Stanley-Mallett

Part II of this book is the fourth co-published by myself and my husband. It is I believe a closer and more unified work. The longer one writes and the older one gets so understanding increases.

The book follows my own publication of *The Door,* which I hope some of you found of interest. As a husband-and-wife team, we believe the verse we provide complements and merges. You, the reader, are the judge.

Elizabeth Stanley-Mallett

All poems are original and previously unpublished.

Part I

A Masquerade of Verse

By

Keith Stanley-Mallett

CONTENTS

Love Perseveres	13
Fabric of Time	14
With All	15
Little Miss Contrary	16
Slow the Day to Rise	17
Spirit of Choice	18
Only Time	19
The Windowpane	20
How Passes Time!	21
Autumnally Born	22
The Prediction	23
Timeless Tears	24
A Moment of Reality	25
Born	26
Like a Lure	27
Tins	28
Winter Surprises	29
Arrows of the Mind	30
The Sky	31
December	32
Reality	33
The Passing Years	34
Gently All	35
The Image	36
Humanity's Mask	37
Hallowed Days	38
Poo!	39
Old Is	40
Gilded Images	41
As a Spider Weaves	42
Sugar Rime	43
Witches' Brooms	44
Ale, Wine or Spirit	45

The Starmen	46
In Skies of Blue	47
Evening Clouds	48
This Nation	49
The Gilded Days	50
Everlasting Home	51
Little Yellow Cottage	52
Eternal Ages	53
By His Hand and Name	54
February's Face	55
No Shield	56
Essence of Morning	57
Passing Years	58
The Sting	59
Of Singular Colour	60
Almost Famous	61
Lord of All	62
Liberty	63
Wild Air	64
Wily Hunters	65
Summer Days	66
Weaving Threads	67
Spirit of the Age	68
Fire in the Hearth	69
A Quiet Embrace	70
The Right Course	71
The Whole	72
Communicator	73
The Truth	74
Such a Hurry	75
Divided	76
Urgent Reality	77
Summer Solstice	78
For Life, for Earth, for Man	79

Love Perseveres

So quickly gone are happy times,
    So quickly gone the years
Since we married that September
    Yet, love still perseveres.

Although our youth is long since past
    And we are deemed as old,
Still the spirit of life and love
    Runs true, free and bold.

In thought and deed we complement
    We share our knowledge bound,
And still we seek the secrets
    Of love and life profound.

Fabric of Time

When the fabric of time
    Is torn asunder,
Then will there be
    Such infinite wonder.
The primeval birth of life
    To the mighty dinosaurs,
World climate changes
    Where volcanic lava pours.
Heaving mountains lift and rise
    Seas roar to places new,
Lands and forests changing, as
    The years to millennia grew.

The earth convulsed, to view,
    Deserts and ice full spread,
And in their time commanded
    Each region in lifeless dread.
To witness aeons of ages
    Geological changes,
The rise and fall of empires
    Listen to oracles and sages.
So through all history
    Its sights and tragedies
Upheavals, the good and bad,
    The wonder of time's images.

With All

So here we are
    In life, uncounted,
The human race
    Spirit unbounded.
In all its guises
    Traits and passions,
Wars and wonders
    Progress and fashion.
Multiplicity
    Of race and tongue,
Working, striving
    In cold lands and sun.

Year by passing year
    On into the future,
Eyes open to some
    Blindness others endure.
Up the net of time
    Into the unknown,
With curses and laughter
    In being we have grown.
Full understanding
    Perhaps, yet attain
Of life's purpose,
    With all we lose and gain.

Little Miss Contrary

Little Miss Contrary
    Like unto a fairy,
With a mind so flighty
    Changing day and nightly.
Skipping home from school
    Some things she said were cruel,
Such tales extraordinaire
    Wild stories she did dare.

She did not tell a lie
    Yet truth she did deny,
How or why, where or with
    Was fun to her, what she did.
Little Miss Contrary
    Like unto a fairy,
Naughty in her mischief
    Contraire, her air and brief.

Slow the Day to Rise

The early morning mist
Hangs over field and village,
Bequeathing a shadowy light
    Veiled by a wet, still cage.

Such an autumnal morning
Depicting half-clothed trees,
Water drops hang suspended
    While underfoot lie yellowed leaves.

Still, quiet and dew-soaked
Lies the ground beneath grey cloud,
Slow will be the day to rise
    Through the enclosing shroud.

Spirit of Choice

To live or not live,
    Die or not to die,
To dream or not dream
    Sigh, or not to sigh.

Such are life's emotions
    Wrought upon our being,
Day by day will bind us
    Through the years of living.

Children to maturity
    Early laughter, singing,
The joy and the sadness
    Time brings a-winging.

Yet beyond such thoughts
    There lies within, a voice,
Of conscience and reason,
    The spirit of choice.

Only Time

When you study history
    And look at the world today,
Disregarding innovations
    Progress is still at bay.
We have not learned collectively
    To listen, to share, to trust
Each other respectfully
    Which humanity surely must.
Only time will tell
    If humanity matures,
Or forever remains
    To childishly endure
The same old conflicts
    Through diverse ideology,
Narrowly thought-out teaching
    Wrought from bad philosophy.
Yet someday we will know
    The wrongs and rights of life,
A blending of minds to see
    A future without strife.

The Windowpane

Once more I sit before the glass
To see another autumn scene
Beyond the windowpane,
    The views of meadows green.
Bounded by the hedgerows lean,
Whose summer coverlets
Have left each shrub and tree,
    To show the bones at rest.
Painted in pale gold, yet shadow'd,
Light floods the still, damp land,
Where ponies graze the meadow
    Below a sky of blue, whose hand –
Of nature's artist, blends soft cloud
With sunlight's soft radiance,
All in this quiet autumnal place
    Pause in restful dalliance.
For as I sit once more to view
Did the glass before me frame
A picture, as though painted
    Beyond the windowpane?

How Passes Time!

Christmas again
    How time passes!
Chill the wine
    Get out the glasses.

Bright glows the tree
    Fairy lights winking,
Cards on display
    Tinsel a-twinkling.

Guests arriving,
    Carol singing,
Smell of dinner
    Spirits winging.

Presents to give
    Thoughts to remind,
Christmas again
    How passes time!

Autumnally Born

Today is grey
Clouds touch the ground,
Creating fog
    Muffling sound.

Dreary and wet
Blanketing light,
Vision impaired
    Nothing in sight.

Water droplets
Hang suspended,
And all about
    Naturally blended.

Persistent mist
Of hydrous form,
Overlaying all
    Autumnally born.

The Prediction

Will we all be here
After two thousand and twelve?
    For rumour and old writings
    State we all shall be felled.
Ending of a calendar,
While mystics say the earth
    Will turn about its axis,
    Upheavals round its girth.

The planets will line up
With the galaxy centre,
    Magnetic pull aligned
    Could possibly upend her,
Thus, thrown about like skittles
And broken upon its face,
    Could well predict the end
    For all the human race.

Timeless Tears

Through the darkness
    Of early hours,
    The rain falls as a
    Soft-voiced shower.
Parting the clinging mist
    That hangs a veil,
    Screening the morn,
    This November, pale.
Until the grey of dawn
    Advanced un-bright
    The day, bereft
    Of morning sunlight.
So continues this morn
    'Twixt rain and mist,
    With timeless tears
    The earth is kissed.

A Moment of Reality

A pause, a thought,
    A feeling of fate,
A moment only
    To contemplate.

That singular touch
    So mystifying,
Of unknown and known
    Truth, yet denying –

The presence of time,
    For one brief moment
You felt reality,
    And all it meant.

Born

Out of silent nothingness,
Beyond all memory
And consciousness
    Burst the incendiary –

Of violent concussion,
Following explosion
Abruptly detonated
    Into this space chosen.

Such noisome sound,
Fireborn blasted energy
Awoke the darkness
    With violent urgency.

Spilling piercing light,
Igniting the depths
The netherspace unbound,
    Creation born, form and breath.

Like a Lure

It's that time again!
    The crowding through the doors,
The rush to each department
    Of the high-street store.
Aglow with coloured lights
    And the season's decorations,
Stock arranged attractively
    Perhaps to change inclinations
The minds of jostling shoppers,
    As they search for gifts
Rising floor to floor
    In the crowded lifts.
Festive music in the air
    Acts like a lure, sweet as honey,
Hurry, hurry, buy, buy,
    It's Christmas, and we want your money.

Tins

Such a strange desire,
Out of all the things
There are to choose from,
    You happen upon tins.

Old tins and new ones
Large, small, tall or short
Picturesque or embossed
    No matter where bought.

Scenes of long ago
Colourful romantic,
Country cottages,
    Castles fantastic –

To old-fashioned
Victorian shops,
Fronts a-glitter,
    Snow on rooftops.

Or bright-red buses,
The passengers seen,
In a London street
    With lamps agleam.

Cake tins, sweets and tea,
Biscuit and more there be,
Picturesque or embossed
    Colourful to see.

Winter Surprises

The Ice Queen's fairy folk
    Have been out and about,
Skipping across the meadows
    For there can be no doubt,
Ice dusting every stalk,
    Powdering field and tree
Glittering crystal white,
    By starlight pale, they see –

To weave intricate patterns
    Etched on windowpanes,
While spiders' webs are turned
    Into threads of silver chain.

Lake and pond reflect the stars
    In their frozen-water form,
Mirrors of the winter night
    A time when frost is born,
Water elementals
    In all their diverse guises,
Touch and change all things
    And sometimes, surprises.

Arrows of the Mind

The sharp arrows of the mind
Can dart this way and that,
Or truly aimed can pierce
    Such distant realms, a fact –

Within the mind to reach
New understanding, wrought
To tear the shadow'd veil
    By the power of thought.

Thus the light of knowledge
Reaches out, to pursue
Yet, 'twas the very arrows
    Of those, who sought the truth.

The Sky

Such clarity of sight
    I can see through the sky,
So clear is the air
    That now even I,
Can be like a bird
    It's as though I can fly,
Reach out to infinity
    Way beyond, so high,
Is it to this great height
    My spirit goes, when I die?
Then again my mind plays
    With ideas, the why,
Indulging in fantasy
    As I gaze into the sky.

December

I love the last of seasons,
    Each December, its sign,
With the trees outlined
    Against a twilit skyline.

I embrace the mystic hours
    The crisp clear fresh air,
The colour of the sky
    The early stars that share –

The beauty of an evening,
    As it draws to a close
The end of another year,
    With its early sunset glows.

I stand beneath the sky
    Betwixt here and now of time,
And I understand the nature
    That December can define.

Reality

Is there a Great Father
Or only reality?
A protective spirit
    Or is this just fantasy?

Teachers there were of old
Who gave us our laws,
Taught us how to live
    Yet taught us also war.

Wherefore is the spirit?
The guidance and the love,
Harmony, tranquillity
    The light from above.

There remains reality,
The world in which we live,
Wild nature and beauty
    All it has to give.

Knowledge we have gained
Science, space, humanity,
All that we comprehend
    Remains reality.

The Passing Years

Days go by as quick as thoughts
    The weeks, the months, the years,
So follows the seasons' changes
    Happiness wrought, fear or tear.

So quickly do the years pass
    One cannot quite keep up,
From childhood through to maturity
    Past and present corrupts –

The very minds of young and old,
    Condensing all the living days
That youth and older folk require,
    To live the life that they –

In their total innocence
    They believe is justly theirs,
But time speeds fast on by
    Ignoring earthly cares.

And so days, weeks and months
    The yearly passing seasons,
Condenses and corrupts
    Giving no valid reason.

Gently All

Slow the snow,
    Silent found
Crystal flakes,
    Drifting down
From above
    This grey morn,
Where on high
    They were born.
All a-dance
    Gently all,
From heaven
    To earth, fall.
'Tis nature's
    Own reason,
For snowflakes
    This season.

The Image

The image of Father Christmas,
The spirit of goodwill,
Abounds in colourful costume
    The season's stockings to fill.

You see him in the stores,
You see him on the street,
You see him on Christmas cards
    In pictures of snow and sleet.

The epitome of Yuletide
With his bulging sack of gifts,
Together with twinkling trees
    Holly and mistletoe lifts –

The heart, mind and spirit
Above the cold winter drear,
To make this festive time
    One of love, hope and good cheer.

Humanity's Mask

Humanity is unstable,
Their conditioning is cast,
Too long the psychology
    Instilled from the past.

Human diversity
Becomes a troublesome task,
Ideology and religion
    All humanity's mask.

Infused down the ages
And thus wrought to last,
Race and gender taught
    Not to question or ask.

So quick the anger and hate,
Unbelieving, refusing to grasp
We should all work together,
    Not hide behind a mask.

Hallowed Days

Those hallowed days in winter
    Though desperately few,
Are as soothing balm
    'Twixt the old year and new.
Days of cheer and merriment
    Friends once more united,
Feasting and the parties
    Lamps and candles lighted.
Yet, also a time for rest
    For thought and contemplation,
A pause to remember
    Past times and relations.
Those few days in winter
    With their magical powers,
Banish life's cares awhile
    For pleasant festive hours.

Poo!

A dog he goes a-wooing
    To court his doggy lass,
He also goes a-pooing
    And leaves it on the grass.
Although he is a lovely pet
    And is a joy to own,
He has his doggy habits
    Which are his and his alone.
In the garden he does roam
    Sniffing at this and that,
Then chases all the birds
    And tries to catch the cat.
He is a cuddly beast
    A furry friend and true,
But I wish he wouldn't leave
    His little presents of poo!

Old Is

When all the years have flown
Old is as old feels,
For better or worse
    With the aches and the ills.

Depending on one's age.
Style of modern life,
Health, habits and mind
    To subdue any strife –

Do the years fall for you
Like a dark shadow hovers,
Making life painful and hard
    And life becomes a bother?

Or is the spirit still
Within the beating heart,
Accepting the flow of time
    To cushion the years in part?

So with wisdom life enjoy,
Although the aches remain
And ills confine you more,
    Old is as old does claim.

Gilded Images

An image that brings joy,
    A fine painting hung,
Painted by an artist
    Under a golden sun.
Or a view of the countryside
    Woodlands and green meadows.
An old quaint cottage
    Where climbing roses grow.

A theatre performance
    With the players and lights,
An orchestral evening
    Brings music into flight.
Visions that give such
    Deep-set expression,
These are the images
    The gilded impression.

As a Spider Weaves

A spider spinning true his web
Concentrating on his task,
Spins his sticky silken thread
    Around and round 'til at last
Completes the spreading trap,
Then retreats just out of sight
One leg upon a thread, he sat
    To await his victim's plight.

Reminding me of humanity,
Of greed and cruelty on
Those who can't escape the finality
    Of the perpetrator's gun and bomb.
They weave their tricky plans
Uncaring of others' fate,
The evil woven by their hands
    Will only stir up hate.

Sugar Rime

The land is a giant cake,
    A Christmas or birthday cake,
With its surface ice-white
    Be it land, lane or lake.

A crystalline surface
    Frozen in form for a time,
As if a large brush
    Painted with sugar rime.

Bright to the eye, it gleams,
    Frost-formed by night
A true winter scene,
    Sparkling in sunlight.

Witches' Brooms

Upon the skyline near and far
The black outline of thrusting trees
    Stark and gaunt like witches' brooms,
    Quite menacing appear to me.

Beneath the brooding clouds of grey
That hang like a veil of shadows
    Over cottage and woodland, falls
    Dismal and dark on the meadow.

No song is heard from any bird,
No rabbit, hare or fox is seen,
    And cattle huddle by the hedge
    In this morning's dreary scene.

A day of damp, heavy-laden
Between the earth and cloud up high,
    Only fit for witches' brooms
    Thrusting darkly to the sky.

Ale, Wine or Spirit

When the labour of day is done
And mind and body pause for rest,
Hands and thoughts retreat from work
    For food, ale or spirit to ingest.
For man has need of more than food,
Ale and spirits feed the mind,
Can help in diverse situations
    Or calm in fateful times.

Yet man is as man does, too much
Some abuse the body's liver,
Overindulge and a drunk become
    Their health and life do not consider.

To others drink can be a friend
Helping to sustain at moments of stress,
Bolster one's courage, steel the nerves
    When danger arrives to test!
But the greatest pleasure of all
Is to lift a glass of your desire,
Whether ale, wine or spirit
    To savour life, quietly by the fire.

The Starmen

When the Starmen saw the earth
From the great everlasting void,
They saw a rich and living home
    With treasures, they could enjoy.

Across the vastness of space
They came to seek and live,
With servants from another race
    Their labours made to give.

They built their vast stone cities
Primitive humanoids they changed to man
And taught him awareness,
    Yet faults they brought upon the land.

The worst of these was war,
Teaching men how to fight,
How to kill and destroy
    Instead of teaching what was right.

With their powerful weapons
Jealousies and childish hate,
They destroyed their own cities
    Leaving few to their fate.

Man was left to live alone
Upon a strange mythical world,
Secrets lost and secrets kept
    The banner of wisdom, now unfurled.

In Skies of Blue

The birds fly high in skies of blue
    Yet low in skies of grey,
The spirits soar in days of sun
    When drear, do lowly lay.

'Tis the mark of all such creatures
    For all are bound the same,
Even our own emotions, are tied
    To nature's precocious ways.

As the sun does many things,
    Lightens and lifts the air,
Removing the heaviness
    Which all on dismal days do share.

So when the sun does brightly shine
    In a sky clear and blue,
Each bird with joy, high will fly
    Each spirit of nature, true.

Evening Clouds

The golden platter dips below
The darkening horizon's skyline,
Like liquid gold poured forth
    Upon the evening clouds to shine,
Like coloured velvet in the glow
Of firelight's flickering flames,
With ruby red and corn-fresh yellow
    As day and sunset wane,
With changing rainbow hues
Until twilight softly falls,
And light of day gives way
    To night's own starlit halls.

This Nation

England, a country once free and true
    A land defended by the brave,
Who gave their lives for the red, white and blue
    Now this England has become a slave.

A servant of bureaucracy
    Pandering to ideology,
Swamped by foreign nationals
    Weak, her dealing with criminology.

So sad to see this attitude,
    I'm disgusted with this nation
Where its leaders' hands are tied,
    Whatever happened to determination!

The stupidity of modern laws
    Such crass thinking by faceless fools,
I hope to God they don't succeed
    And we never surrender to foreign rules.

The Gilded Days

So quick the gilded days
    Swiftly pass in life,
First of all golden time
    Were of youth, young and lithe.

Then came times of romance
    Summer evenings warmly felt,
When feelings quite unknown
    Ruled body, heart and self.

So on to maturity,
    To wisdom learned,
A time of understanding
    Secure in what you've earned.

Lastly, the quiet day's
    Retirement from the rush,
Time for contemplation
    To sleep in sunshine's blush.

Everlasting Home

When your time nears its end
    And it's your turn to die,
Will your spirit up and go?
    Does it up and fly?

Do we become an entity
    Unseen, unheard, unreal?
Can we still see and hear
    Speak, touch, smell and feel?

Is it possible do you think
    For others of like, to visit?
Or one's own relations
    To know again in spirit?

Is there a plane of existence
    Where living energy does go?
To once again know friends and pets
    An everlasting home.

Little Yellow Cottage

There's a little yellow cottage
One of three down the lane,
And it sits by the woodland
    Where the cottage got its name.
Across the lane the hedgerows run
With berry, hip and haw,
Around the back the spinney stands
    Beyond the garden door.

Horses graze upon the meadows
Behind the rustic fence,
Left, past the standing oak
    A nursery to complement.

Whilst the views from front and rear
Scan the countryside afar,
Fields of corn and vegetables
    Geese, duck and song of lark.
A cottage in the country
A cottage from the past,
A little yellow cottage
    A cottage built to last.

Eternal Ages

The years roll onward
Ever onward, onward,
And all of us, humanity
    Are tied as if by cord
To a minute of time.
One moment of feeling,
One moment of living
    Conscious of being.

No time to discern
Endless reality,
To understand oneself
    Or reason to be?
Swiftly flow the years
The eternal ages' song,
Each spark of life
    No sooner lit, than gone.

By His Hand and Name

The sea forgives its own,
    River and pond comply,
As all in raw nature
    On the ground and in the sky.
No animosity
    By tooth, claw or beak
Felt towards the hunted,
    Only for sustenance seek.
One creature, known as man
    Lives outside nature's law,
Who, throughout all of time
    Has carried a mental flaw.
He also kills for gain,
    Destruction, anarchy,
All by his hand and name
    As described by history.
Should we forgive our own
    And all that's gone before?
Will we find the answer
    To stop man going to war?

February's Face

January at last has flown
And February steps into place,
Yet it is a harsher month
    For it shows a cold-light face.

Silver-bright is the landscape,
Crystal frosting covers all,
Ice-cold the air, pond and lake
    The sun a glowing opal.

'Til flurry on flurry, the snow
Blankets all from sight,
Fast-falling, swirling, dancing,
    Painting the countryside white.

February's sharp introduction
Reminds us, winter has a long arm,
Bringing such weather, to quickly
    Change the landscape's charm.

No Shield

Knife, sword, bullet,
    Shell, rocket and bomb,
    Are such a diverse array
    To court death's own song.
Each has its own way
    To quickly take life,
    Be it a son or daughter
    A husband or wife.

If it be war
    As a battlefield,
    Then to death many succumb
    For they have no shield.
Now destruction
    With godlike nuclear fission,
    May erase so many
    In a nightmare vision.

Essence of Morning

The silence of the morning
    Is broken only,
By the sound of a dog's
    Barking voice, urgent, lonely.
The sound carries vibrantly
    On the mist-laden air,
Sending a small flock of birds
    To flight, nervously aware.

The essence of the morning
    Embracing a pearl-grey sky,
Is devoid of colour
    As discerned by the eye.
When light from the sun
    Is filtered by deep cloud,
    It masks the natural hues
    And enhances a mist-caught sound.

Passing Years

When the years of youth have gone
    And middle-age too has passed,
    You find yourself so suddenly,
    Frighteningly, now cast
Adrift in a world diverse
    From one where you did excel,
    A world less understood and worse,
    For now you are old as well.

Aches and pains accompany you
    Each day and night, week and month,
    The joy of living, loving,
    Happiness that was known once
Has now deserted, leaving you
    Alone, lost, wondering where
    Loved ones have gone, all is change?
    You are left alone, to stare!

The Sting

Pain is the essence of evil
    To the human spirit,
    Attacking wantonly
    And so inconsiderate.
Causing such hurt to the mind
    Through pathways that reveal
    When all is not right, 'tis then
    The sting of our ills we feel.
Whether wounds, ills or age
    This malevolence we cannot purge,
    Pain from whatsoever source
    Remains such a dreadful scourge.

Of Singular Colour

The morning is made of sugar-ice,
White strings, white tendrils festoon
The fingers of plants, bush and tree,
    As they hang in hoar-frost bloom.

So bright the day, the freezing air
Hangs a covering mist to blend
Each ice-white crystal of frosted snow,
    Blending a morning to comprehend.

A morning of singular colour,
All and every part emerging,
Giving to the eye the spirit
    Pure as a created virgin.

A sugar-ice morning, profound,
Of delicate sculptures, frost-sealed,
Where landscape and sky confound
    By artistry of nature, revealed.

Almost Famous

One thinks one is a writer
    And writes all sorts of things,
Novelettes to novels long
    That they, to fame will bring.

Poetry and essays form
    Articles in magazines,
Yet 'tis of such little note
    The world takes of your writings.

I am nearly almost famous
    For the work I had published,
A poem here a poem there.
    A book or two accomplished –

So little fame or credit,
    Yet I know I have the making
Of a writer of repute,
    This literary path I'm taking.

With pen in hand I gaze
    At all that is blameless,
For nature does not care
    Whether or not I'm famous.

Lord of All

Swiftly fly the minutes, hours,
Days turn into weeks,
There is no end to passing time
    As the years repeat.

Time in uncontrollable
It has no substance,
Neither is it energy
    Or spirit to enhance.

It cannot be understood
Why such time exists,
Presenting true reality
    However it persists.

Century follows century
Into aeons do fall,
Time! We cannot master
    It is the lord of all.

Liberty

It is a basic conception,
We all seek for liberty,
A long and timeless struggle
    Throughout all history.
We need to have our freedom,
Ruled by democracy,
Yet still there is a shadow
    A feeling of conspiracy.

Life offers less and less
We have but little choice,
Now many activities
    No longer have a voice.
So much we took for granted
Has been taken or removed,
Liberty has many levels,
    True freedom, must be proved!

Wild Air

Stirred from silent rest
The air to wind was born,
Then agitated so
    Just like a winter storm
It sprang amongst the clouds,
Rushed upon the ground,
Pushing and reaching
    Everything it found.

The trees it caused to dance
To move and sway as one,
Blustering, blowing
    'Til leaves were made to run.
All that could, obeyed
For none could rescind,
The commands of wild air
    When a forceful wind.

Wily Hunters

To follow up an enquiry
Of selected merchandise,
They get in touch by letter
    Or by phone, which is wise.
For once you show an interest
Then you, they'll try to snare,
No matter what the product
    They will lure you to their lair.

They are the wily hunters
In the jungle of today,
The salesman of each product
    Will try to get their way.

They will offer you incentives
Like reductions off the price,
Praise the item of interest
    Then tell you little lies.
Ignore the selling pressure
Buy only what you desire,
For with a little knowledge
    You'll become an adept buyer.

Summer Days

A marmalade of sun
    Bursts across the sky,
    Brilliantly orange
    Spreading far and wide.

Coloured fingers of light
    Seek out each shadowed space,
    Illuminating the day
    Lighting every place.

Spiced with warming rays
    Pervading everywhere,
    The joy of summer days
    Return for all to share.

Weaving Threads

The silver threads of time
    Weave their mystic way,
Upon this world, this earth
    And beyond, to, who can say? –

Where weaving threads of time
    Unite, to present
A universal face
    Of interwoven space, full meant –

As a lowered curtain,
    Bringing a final end
To a woven interspacial
    Time-wrought blend –

Where galactic energy,
    And sun-cast matter die!
Unless in perpetuation
    Silver threads continue life?

Spirit of the Age

When today has passed
And the days that I'm alive,
My time in history,
    The years that we did strive,
When all has gone beyond,
The world changed anew,
What will they think tomorrow
    If the future reviews?

Will we be forgotten
Lost in time's dark halls,
Or will our deeds and life
    Someday be recalled?
The spirit of the age,
The living and endeavour,
Perhaps exists somewhere
    To persist forever.

Fire in the Hearth

When the last of British virtue
Fades in the mists of time,
And the fire in the hearth
Goes out by foreign clime.
Then England herself, is no more!
She has succumbed to those
Whom jealousy has fired,
And trampled underfoot the rose.

Thus for all her sacrifice
Upon the dust her flag will lay,
Her spirit banished from the land
For others will rule the day.

Leaderless, weak, she may flounder
Needing hands of strength,
To reach into the future
With courage and common sense.
Diminished in stature,
Unforthcoming an apology
A state brought about
     By a common ideology.

A Quiet Embrace

There comes such times
    When the sky comes down,
    So quietly
    To kiss the ground.

So unobserved
    It descended with
    Such passion,
    Silent to give –

The swift embrace,
    Of nature's own clasp,
    Between water,
    Air and earth, fast –

Wrought by changes,
    Environment's elements
    Give cause and effect,
    Misty moments.

The Right Course

Far-seeing, a future bleak
    As humanity increases,
    The land will vie with building
    As one expands the other decreases.

The population quickly grows
    And needs constructed housing,
    Such building takes up land
    Which for food should be utilising.

Cities and towns to be built
    Or land for farms endorsed?
    This will be the future problem
    And we must take the right course.

Buildings must go higher
    Reducing the footprint spread,
    Farmland must be protected
    To save our daily bread.

The Whole

Loneliness is emptiness,
Thrust into the unknown,
Last in mind and spirit
Fearful and alone.

Brought a figure, singular,
No more a part of two,
Cast hurtfully aside
So bitterly true.

Thus, like unto an island
Which, in the distance, seen
Small and dark, uncertain
As life, fall shadowy.

This world, this reality
Is not for one, to be,
For two, do make the whole
Within humanity.

Communicator

Sounds the modern messenger
    The mobile phone each day,
    Delivering its message
    By voice from far away.

An alarming sound for some
    Or an awaited call,
    Depending on news then sought
    Would good or bad befall?

Messages flash back and forth
    Winged-Mercury fast,
    Information given
    Offered and asked.

From a mounted messenger
    And the telegram boy,
    Comes this communicator
    This grown-up adult toy.

The Truth

When things go wrong
    In life, as with health,
Problems more serious
    Than money or wealth.

'Tis then the mind begins
    To understand the truth,
That we are not as strong
    As thought, or long in youth.

We are as humans,
    Beings of intent,
Not strong or armoured
    Yet, aware the strength –

Of mind persistent
    To overcome ills,
With determination
    And an iron will –

Together with prayer
    To spiritual gods,
We may overcome
    Such lessening odds.

Such a Hurry

As each day quickly ends
Becoming weeks which pass on by,
Constant adding to the months
    That swiftly seem to fly.

Why is everything
In such a hurry or a fuss?
Night, then day, night, then day
    Alternate times that rush –

Headlong into tomorrow
With unknown futures waiting,
It is as if all is wound
    Within a spring, containing –

A universal energy
That's constantly speeding forward,
Ignoring all that's bound
    As it turns the sphere onward.

Divided

I am not whole!
    To myself alone, confided,
One part removed
    I am divided.

My spirit cleaved
    In atmosphere, thinned
By this suddenness,
    As if by a whim –

Wrought by the gods
    In natural amusement
At life's frailty,
    Tormented, confused.

Thus leaving myself
    Alone, my senses spurned,
Bemused, partnerless,
    Waiting your return.

Urgent Reality

Thus, set within the raw reality
Of life now urgently lived,
Subdued at times with dreamlike quality
Of moments, pleasure filled to give –
An opiate to drug the human mind,
To ease the taxed and overwrought,
And so pleasure give to all humankind
Releasing the burden life has brought.
Yet, but for a singular fleeting moment
Of awareness, the human spirit
Succumbs to reality's torment
Of life, so urgently explicit.

Summer Solstice

The longest day
    Is here to stay
But, for a few hours longer,
    With sun or rain
Summers refrain,
    Her warmth a little stronger.
Moonlit, the night
    Soft as a sigh
Brushed with silken breezes,
    Caresses the mind
And heart to find,
    How summer solstice pleases.

For Life, for Earth, for Man

This mystery of life,
Of cause and effect,
Created energies
    Which receive or reject.

What is this reality
In which humankind
Strives for understanding
    Within each depth of mind?

Constant are the labours
Persistent to exist,
Maintaining civilisation
    With all it consists.

With scientific endeavour
We seek the mystic plan,
The universal meaning
    For life, for earth, for man!

Part II

A Masquerade of Verse

By

Elizabeth Stanley-Mallett

Previously published poems by the same author:
  Guiding Star – Forward Press, 2009
  Winter Sun – Forward Press, 2009
  Beneath Rose-Lemon Skies – Arthur H. Stockwell Ltd, 2009
  A Narrow By-Way – Anchor Books, 2010
  Valentine – Forward Press, 2010
  June Roses – Forward Press, 2010
  Little Green Men – Forward Press, 2010
  Before the Rainbow Fades Part II – Arthur H. Stockwell Ltd, 2010
  Between Night and Dancing Light Part II – Arthur H. Stockwell Ltd, 2010
  Valentine 2010 – Forward Poetry, 2011
  Three to a Seat – Forward Poetry, 2011
  Learners All – Forward Poetry, 2011
  The Door – Arthur H. Stockwell Ltd, 2011

CONTENTS

Golden Waves	87
I've Got the Bug	88
Animal Worth	89
The Wheel of Fortune	90
High Summer	91
Worrying	92
Lullaby	93
The Boys in Blue	94
A New Car	95
The Crock of Gold	96
The Golden Kiss of Autumn	97
What Does Christmas Mean to You?	98
Just Two Minutes	99
Another Day, Another Dollar	100
The Christmas Fairy	101
The Sounding of the Chime	102
Capacity to Forgive	103
Summer Memory	104
It Pours from His Pen	105
The Prisoner	106
On the Shelf	107
Chopping and Changing	108
It's Dark	109
Sell-by Date	110
Are We Stupid?	111
Joint Effort	112
When the Wind Moans	113
The Parting	114
Sinister Shadow	115
My Love	116
Nerves of Steel	117
The Staff of Life	118

The Striking of Thirteen?	119
The Gods Next Door	120
Monarch	121
Yippee!	122
Just Like Rome	123
Fair, Fat and Forty	124
The Nurse	125
Stocktaking	126
Problems	127
Better or Worse	128
Cold, Icy Grip	129
Avalon	130
Fear	131
Death Traps	132
The Spider	133
Little Corporal	134
St Kilda	135
Both Leader and Led	136
Craving	137
A Gaelic Song	138
Universal Fusion	139
Traveller's Joy	140
Jack of All Trades	141

Golden Waves

Ripened fully by the sun
    The fields ripple in the breeze,
To fill the nation's breadbasket
    Habitat of birds and bees.

Planted in early spring
    On East Anglian clay,
Green shoots grew fast to form
    Golden waves on display.

Rainfall though sometimes sparse
    Has finally drenched the fields,
To swell the ears of corn and
    Bless this harvest's yield.

Thanksgiving time then arrives
    The grain is proudly shown,
Golden-baked cottage loaves
    From flour ground on stone.

The fields are ploughed and tilled
    Bereft of the golden grain,
Lying fallow until the spring
    When the cycle begins again.

I've Got the Bug

To write has become addictive
    I've really got the bug,
Pouring out thoughts, my emotions
    Like water from the kitchen jug.

I need to put on paper
    My ideals, aspirations,
Showing up my character
    By insight and revelations.

I give too much away
    Should learn to slow my hand,
Take more time, relax a while
    Building castles in the sand.

But, I am compelled to write,
    I've really got the bug,
Can't stop, must carry on
    Ere time pulls my plug.

That mortal enemy
    Of all human souls,
Much to do, so little time
    To achieve my cherished goals.

Animal Worth

I like the animal programmes
    Like *All Creatures Great and Small*?
Farmers who are so very mean
    Care not for stock at all.

Too mean to feed them properly
    Too mean to call the vet,
Too busy baiting neighbours
    By habits firmly set.

The animals that serve them well
    Products of nature's purse,
They deserve the very best
    Welfare must come first.

The horse that ploughs the field
    Patiently plodding stride,
A warm stable after work
    A nosebag on the side.

The cow in the byre still chewing the cud
    She lets her milk flow free,
Rich in cream and calcium
    Enjoyed by all the family.

And what of cuddly pets?
    Solace to young and old,
A comfort when required
    So, worth their weight in gold.

The Wheel of Fortune

The wheel of fortune spins slowly
    Is it really the wheel of fate,
Mapping out our course in life
    Never fast or late?

We cannot see the future
    Maybe just as well
Good and bad concocted
    Just like a witch's spell.

There are times when life is hard
    So easy to run aground,
Only tenacity will emerge
    Determined strong and sound.

Harm received by a loved one
    Haunts the empathic mind,
You feel you are guilty
    And will be left behind.

The laughter of kids at play
    Fills your day with joy,
Running, tumbling, jumping
    Fiddling with their toys.

Mock wars between children
    Inbred urge to fight,
The wheel of fortune indicates
    Which is wrong and right.

High Summer

It is high summer and so very hot
    The earth is parched and dry,
Not a cloud can be seen
    Drifting across the sky.

The hills cry out for rain
    The valley lake has gone,
The plants scorched and brown
    Under a merciless sun.

Will it ever change?
    When cometh the rain,
Grass roots are dying
    Shrivelled on the plain.

Now we hear thunder
    A welcomed loud clash,
Rain begins to fall
    More than just a splash.

Ears of wheat soak it up
    Swelling the inner grain,
Nature's bounty is restored
    Thanks to summer rain.

Worrying

Why do I sit and worry?
    Why do I sit and brood?
Does not find an answer
    Only darkens my mood.

Problems pile up every day
    Be it bills or daily health,
It makes things worse to worry
    About my state of wealth.

Pay my way, owe not too much
    Spreading out my orders,
Keeps my head above water
    Avoids dire disorders.

Having much to be thankful
    A husband so very dear,
Who sorts out my muddles
    Keeps my thinking clear.

Still I'm a born ponderer
    Enjoying the exercise,
The brain keeps ticking over.
    So one day I'll grow wise.

Lullaby

The mother sat by the cradle
    Crooning a lullaby,
Wanting her baby to sleep
    And cease his plaintive cry.

All night long the cries went on
    Upsetting, annoying and shrill,
What was the matter now?
    Is the baby really ill?

Come the morn, all is quiet
    Rest comes at last,
But the baby is immobile
    No more breath in gasps.

The little one, his spirit
    Hovers above the crib,
Sees mother's tears and
    Is willing to forgive.

She had been impatient
    Worn out, worried and tired,
Had kept on caring still
    Though her strength had expired.

No one can ever comprehend
    How such a loss defies,
Physical limits of all life
    Masked by her lullabies.

The Boys in Blue

I'm mad about the RAF
    Those handsome lads in blue,
I am completely enchanted
    I'll stick with them like glue.

I just cannot help it
    They always fascinate me,
Heroes of every endeavour
    I'm weak at the knee.

How can I explain
    Or attempt to describe,
How tied I am to the
    Cream of England's pride?

When needed they respond
    When wanted they are there,
No other force can reckon with
    These brave lords of the air.

I consider I am fortunate
    As the wife of a serviceman,
Wartime sees their feats of courage
    Since flying first began.

A New Car

My partner's getting a new car
    And yes it's a Chevrolet,
A comfortable, roomy hatchback
    In a lovely shade of grey.

Away will go the blue estate
    Rather too lengthy to turn,
Heavy on fuel consumption
    A costly lesson to learn.

We never did load it up
    For carting household wares,
The new car will serve just as well
    We are pleased to declare.

We have had many Chevys
    In colours of many hues,
Red, green, orange and blue
    Now urban grey is due.

We stick with our chosen make
    Supplied by W. H. Brand,
Whose fair sales and attention are
    Confirmed with a shake of hand.

The Crock of Gold

At the end of a rainbow
    Is found a crock of gold,
    But no one has found it yet
    So the story's told.

Which end of the rainbow
Would reveal the pot?
It's easy to imagine
    The keeper has forgot –

Where he has hidden it
Amongst the pretty bands,
Colours of the rainbow
    Linking sky to land.

Many a hopeful person
Has tried to find the hoard,
Be he serf, knight or king
    Serving wench or lord.

The real crock of gold
Is found in a different way,
Family love and unity
    Always on display.

Disputes are so silly
Childish and immature,
Put it all behind you
    Find the natural cure.

Blood is thicker than water
So we all are told,
In tolerant hearts and minds
    We find our crock of gold.

The Golden Kiss of Autumn

Whirling, skirling, the leaves quit the trees
    Tumbling free, all the way down,
Yellows, reds, orange, hues of russet
    Not just plain shrivelled brown.

Kissed by autumn the landscape basks
    In mellow October light,
Waiting for the chilly winds to strip
    Bare the trees with cold, icy bite.

An Indian summer it's called
    A late few autumn days,
Lurking round the corner winter waits
    To rule once more with freezing ways.

Rosehips bright, full of goodness grown,
    To their hedgerow home they cling,
Food for many feathered friends
    Proud defiance in the gusting winds.

The kiss of autumn soft and gold
    Tarries not, but moves swiftly on,
Soon frost and cold will have their way
    And autumn's kiss will fade anon.

What Does Christmas Mean to You?

What does Christmas mean to you?
    A time of presents and gifts,
Overeating, drinking too much
    With bitter sibling rifts?

Who grabs what or takes the most?
    Gone the art of sharing,
Family groups gathered should
    Find the art of caring.

A time to show, time to display
    Blood is thicker than water,
Grudgingly pass gifts around
    From, Dad to Mum, son to daughter.

Another year has nearly passed
    Another Christmas time,
Peace and harmony on Christmas Eve
    When up the stairs we climb.

A pagan festival of long ago
    Now the Christian nativity,
Story of the Saviour's birth
    Told in plain simplicity.

Just Two Minutes

It seems all we can spare
    Is two minutes of our time,
In respectful silent homage
    To men cut down in their prime.

We may have a busy schedule
    Our lips are sure to quiver,
Their time so cruelly taken
    Will not be returning ever.

They gave much more than minutes
    Proud servicemen in the past,
Their reservoir of life was drained
    By a sacrifice so vast.

Two minutes we stand in silence
    And humbly bow our heads,
As duke and dustman join to
    Salute the men that bled.

Just two minutes of respectful quiet
    Is that all we can give?
We would stand the hours around
    If they once more could live.

Another Day, Another Dollar

Another day, another dollar
    But we much prefer the pound,
Why dabble in foreign currencies
    When we have sterling sound?

We do not need Europe's union
    We can export far and wide,
Countries not shackled by their rules
    To the Commonwealth we relied.

We had a good thing going
    Before we volunteered to fail.
Get out now, pull the plug
    Let the others weep and wail.

Our Tory leader dragged us in
    Without true wisdom thought,
Now at last we can understand
    We were well and truly caught.

Obeying their stupid rules
    Has cost this country dear,
Sensible British people
    Want to get out clear.

Another day, another dollar
    We will stick with our pound,
Prosperity will return again
    When the British make it sound.

The Christmas Fairy

Sparkling silver, she balanced high
    Right on the top of the tree,
Wondering why she was there at all
    Above the glittering scene.

Long packed away in a box
    Stuffed in a dismal loft,
With broken pathetic chains and
    Old clothes chewed by moths.

No one went up to the attic
    From one year to the next,
It was just like the entire house
    Was under the spell of a hex.

Gloom, doom, and spiders' webs
    Bats squeaking in the rafters,
All lay there undisturbed when
    From downstairs there came laughter.

For the lady of the house
    Had a granddaughter fair,
Who liked to run and play
    By the Christmas tree there.

Standing tiptoe on a chair,
    To see the top of the tree,
She espied the shining doll
    The sparkling Christmas Fairy.

The girl cried out with glee
    She thought the doll so beautiful,
Atop of the festive tree
    The fairy felt love shine through.

The Sounding of the Chime

The stroke of midnight heralds
    The magic witching hour,
Fairies, pixies, elves all troop
    From their hidden mystic bowers.

Shoemaker, out of leathers
    Was aided by tiny gnomes,
Their fine quality work
    Was wanted in every home.

The shoemaker prospered
    Thanks to midnight's stroke,
He owed a mighty debt
    To the little helpful folk.

Rumplestiltskin was not of that ilk
    Reluctant his name to share,
Chanting it, he was overheard
    By the miller's daughter fair.

Outraged he stamped his tiny foot
    As hard as he could,
Unaware he said his name
    Louder than he should.

As the stroke of midnight tolls,
    The pendulum of time
Swings on, the day to end
    By the sounding of the chime.

Capacity to Forgive

In a few of us lies a quality,
    The capacity to forgive
Hurtful transgressions
    That mar the way we live.

Do we bear a grudge, seek revenge
    On the perpetrators many
Who burgle homes, desecrate
    Or leave us without a penny?

It takes great courage and bravery
    To turn the other cheek,
Acts of compassion often seen
    As belonging to the weak.

Just the opposite is true
    Forgive very hard to do,
The numbers of such people
    Amount to very few.

Giving others a second chance
    Can bring a mixed reward,
Either you change their ways
    Or take such hurt on board.

Summer Memory

Defying the chilly, biting wind
    To the beech hedge the leaves still cling,
Waiting for winter to pass and
    The timely arrival of spring.

Dejected, a rosebud hangs its head
    Unfulfilled summer memory,
Unsightly, dried-up petals, too
    Ashamed to grace its tree.

Few remaining hips and haws
    Glow brightly on the shrub,
Attracting migrant birds
    Probing every minute stub.

Winter grip holds fast
    As the season moves along,
Summer memory wiped out
    Yet for some, lingers on.

Beech leaves will grow again
    The rose bush sprout anew,
When next the springtime comes
    With colours of every hue.

It Pours from His Pen
(A tribute to Keith)

It could be any time, day or night
    Does it really matter when?
The sheer entertainment
    Just pours from his pen.

Sitting in front of his window
    At the desk in his den,
Works on diverse subjects
    Just pour from his pen.

Be it space, nature, politics
    As it was, now and then,
Poetry, on wars and families
    Written down by his pen.

For sheer quantity of work
    Many times by ten,
Incomparable quality
    Just pours from his pen.

It will be placed with other
    Great poetical works of men,
Still, his poems keep on flowing
    And pouring from his pen.

The Prisoner

Perfectly concealed by the greenery
    High in the blasted oak,
Sat a gaudy parakeet
    Who just loved to gloat.

Once he had been a prisoner
    In a fancy cage,
Property of a parson
    A product of a bygone age.

Now in the oak he saw below
    Inside the ruined church,
His old master had no idea that
    He was up there on a perch.

The parson knelt down to pray
    Thought about his bird,
Who had flown away one day
    And since had never been heard.

He had coaxed the bird to talk
    Although very little it spoke,
If only he had known
    It sat there in the oak

Not far away, but above his head.
    He looked at the empty cage,
He heard the sound of flight and
    Stunned, he was amazed.

There before his very eyes
    He shouted out in his glee,
His pet was back and well
    Its cage no longer empty.

On the Shelf

There is such a vast range
    Of things, on many a shelf,
Like tins of paint and tools
    A garden gnome and elf.

There is another meaning
    To being on the shelf,
An aging, lonely spinster
    Regardless of her wealth.

In the village local store
    Goods are on display,
Attracting all the buyers
    By their tempting array.

The library's many books
    Neatly, shown in rows,
Readers browse idly through
    Reaching the highs and lows.

In the chemist's shop
    Hoards of various drugs,
Stolen by villains and
    Sold on the street to mugs.

On the homestead mantelpiece
    Christmas cards on the shelf,
Greetings of peace, tranquillity
    Happiness and good health.

Chopping and Changing

People that always chop and change
    Are reliably inconsistent,
One wonders if they
    Have a built-in resistance –

To decision-making or truth,
    Dither, dither, here and there,
Which way will be best?
    Truth or facts to share.

It is the same with partners
    Always something wrong,
Yet nobody is perfect
    So, why not stick to one?

To some it is exciting
    Chopping and changing,
Such an artificial life
    It sorely needs arranging.

When the chips are down
    On them you can't depend,
So, no one is willing
    To be called their friend.

It's Dark

When I get up in the morning
    Outside is so dark,
Makes me feel depressed
    I cannot rise with the lark.

The day is dull and grey
    Sunshine rays are rare,
Short hours of daylight
    Too soon we're back upstairs.

No time to get much done
    So very little light,
Birds have ceased their chirping
    Quietened by the night.

Time we are all in bed
    Quickly after we start,
Pull across the curtains
    No surprise, it's dark.

I wish I had a tinderbox
    Just to create a spark,
And light a thousand candles
    To illuminate the dark.

Sell-by Date

I re-entered the romance market
    But it was rather late,
There is no doubt about it
    I'm past my sell-by date.

The ravages of life took their toll
    I'm unsteady on my feet,
At least my mental faculties
    Are more or less complete.

Like many packets of food
    Not much time to go,
Ere the date arrives when
    To the bin we throw.

Little span of time is left
    Not very long to wait,
I've had an intriguing life
    Up to my sell-by date.

My descendants will gain bequests
    As left in my estate,
Let's hope they can benefit
    Before their sell-by dates.

Are We Stupid?

Are we being stupid
    Or are we just thick
When we overeat
And make ourselves sick?

Are we being stupid
    Obeying EU rules?
There can be no doubt
We sure are silly fools.

Are we being stupid
    Driving through the night
When eyes become quite heavy
And so impair our sight?

Are we being stupid
    When we fill our shopping bags
With sale's gaudy bargains?
Just apologies for rags.

It's just the same with food
    Stupid eat-by date,
We cannot possibly consume
Which means we throw away.

Joint Effort

It's not a cut of meat
Nor a carpenter's dovetailed joint,
When Keith and I cooperate
    To present our rhyming points.

We enjoy the work together
Putting into poetic form,
Views on life in general
    In sunshine and in storm.

A thought comes into our heads
And takes shape on the page,
Writings of fact and fiction
    Develop stage by stage.

We try to show the world outside
What we think is wrong,
Deploring acts of weakness
    Wanting leaders to be strong.

The knocks of life quite often
Our ideas impede and thwart,
So, we are delighted with
    Fresh inspirations, that we sought.

When the Wind Moans

When the wind moans in the rafters
    Just what are we hearing?
Spirits of times from long ago
    No wonder we are a-fearing.

Of souls in torment, trapped in limbo
    Unable to let go their crimes,
Caught on a carousel
    Having to relive their crimes.

Is there mercy for these ghosts?
    Can they finally break free?
Compassion coming in the morning
    From the Lord of land, air and sea.

When the wind moans in the rafters
    Not always tormented souls,
Just the mischievous pipes of Pan
    Whistling tunes around the holes.

There is no need to quiver
    Or indulge irrational fears,
It's only the wind in the rafters
    Haunting to our ears.

The Parting

A hurtful division of hearts
    Going their separate ways,
Love that is painfully lost
    Broken 'til the end of days.

Need it always be final?
    Can time find ways to mend?
It only needs regretful words
    For the parting so to end.

Who will admit they're wrong?
    Not many can be brave,
It is worth a little effort
    A relationship to save.

Making up so therapeutic
    Turning lives all around,
Do not harp on past mistakes
    Standing defiantly, your ground.

Perhaps it is a time of sorrow
    Particularly for those who care,
But there is the light-hearted meaning
    Just simple styling of the hair.

Sinister Shadow

A simple device to tell the time
    The shadow falls on the dial,
Depicting swiftly passing hours
Unable to tarry a while.

Like a sinister shadow
    Shading each sunlight ray,
As if a battle 'twixt life and death
Is fought each night and day.

Some see a garden ornament
    Not the sinister shadow,
Time's arrow will be notched
Waiting the release to go.

Better to ignore the darkening past
    Like a herald of impending doom,
Remember the sunshine comes
To melt away the gloom.

So there is no need to fear
    The shadow as it's cast,
Unless your guilty conscience
Conceals a shady past.

My Love

My love is in full view of me
Sitting in the green armchair,
It is a source of comfort
    Just to know he is there.

We have faced many hard times
Our bond is firm and strong,
There can be no doubt
    Together we belong.

Now it's the middle of February
The month of Valentine,
You are my beloved
    I trust I am thine.

The usual drivel is said
About hearts of true,
I can truthfully say
    I belong to you.

We will survive the years
Supporting one the other,
My husband, dear to me
    You're tops as my lover.

Nerves of Steel

A property few of us possess
Quite opposite to what we feel,
How we long, in times of stress
    To have nerves of steel.

The fireman, has to conquer fear
Enter a building on fire,
In spite of all his courage
    The outcome can be dire.

The marksman, trained to shoot
His target, hiding from sight,
Bravely, he aims his gun
    To end a day-long fight.

All of them, kept fear at bay
Did not show how they did feel,
So much is owed to their like
    They deserve a worthy deal.

Recognition of bravery
Of men who fear conceal,
Humbly, we hand our gongs
    After harrowing scenes, so real.

The Staff of Life

The staff of life
More commonly known as bread,
The staple food of all concerned
    By which whole armies were fed.

In Bible days, the parable
Of the loaves and fishes,
Shows the importance
    Of this humblest of dishes.

Without it we cannot live
Protein, starch and bran,
Ingredients found in the loaf
    The basic food of man.

Peasant and lord baked their bread
In kitchen ovens fired by wood,
The resulting crisp, brown wedge
    Smelled and tasted good.

It is a simple pleasure
To consume bread and cheese,
Outside the ploughman ate
    Under the hedgerow lees.

The Striking of Thirteen?

It's said to be a bad omen
Should the clock strike thirteen,
Few of us can have a clue
    Exactly what it means.

It could herald some event
A forthcoming calamity,
So annoying to find out
    We just have to wait and see.

It could be the closing
Of some ancient gate,
Only time will tell
    What will be our fate.

Perhaps there is no need to worry
If the clock strikes thirteen,
It may be just a hiccup
    In the brakes of the machine.

At night, when tired we fall asleep
And our mind begins to dream,
We simply do not hear
    The striking of thirteen.

The Gods Next Door

Long before the dawn of history
Before any cities or law,
Aliens landed on this planet
    And could be living next door.

Robbing the earth of resources
Plundering more and more,
They seem to live for ever and
    Appeared to thrive on war.

We do not recognise these monsters
But just accept they are there,
We were brainwashed entirely
    Though some, their knowledge, shared.

How can we all be so blind
Not seeing they are so close,
Elevated by us as gods
    When we're the ones to lose?

Wake up mankind and see
For they are right next door,
Pushing us this way and that
    Like they did in days of yore!

Monarch

William the Conqueror held the land
    In an iron-fisted grip,
Brought in his Norman lords
Cracking their greedy whips.

He, carried out a census
    Recorded in the Domesday Book,
Which exists to this day
For some to have a look.

The country has a monarchy
    And old traditions handed down,
King John lost in the Wash
His golden, cherished crown.

Queen Elizabeth 1st
    Finally reached the throne,
She refused to pick a consort
And chose to rule alone.

King Charles lost the throne
    And managed to lose his head,
The country ended up the worse
When Cromwell ruled instead.

Under Victoria,
    A South African war,
An end-of-century affair
When the enemy was the Boer.

Now we have Elizabeth
    Long-serving to date,
Now, her jubilee year
It's time to celebrate.

Yippee!

Colin has joined our staff
    After years of staying away,
We are all so delighted
Far more than we can say.

Now, against all the odds,
    Back is young CP,
Our first engineer
It just had to be.

A hearty welcome
    From our happy throng,
There can be no doubt
You're back where you belong.

We are moving up the scale
    One of the top three,
Together we will all shout
Yippee! Yippee!

Who will be the next?
    That is the query,
Liabilities not welcomed
However good their CV.

Happy news at last
    Has come to the family,
Working hard together
A future bright to see.

Just Like Rome

The legions came to Britain
In Julius Caesar's reign,
They found the warring tribes
    Most difficult to tame.

Tribe Iceni had a queen
Boudicca was her name,
She waged a constant fight
    Became a famous name.

Gradually, they built their villas
And cities just like Rome,
All was abandoned when
    The legions were recalled home.

During the occupation
They put up Hadrian's Wall
With forts and towers
    Living quarters for all.

Many Anglo-Romans
Lived in splendid homes,
Not really missing
    The glory that was Rome.

Fair, Fat and Forty

It's OK to reach here
The dreaded milestone of forty,
Keep your sense of humour
    Think of something naughty.

Why worry about being fair?
Life is not like that,
Life's little nasty habit
    Turns everything to fat!

What is really important
Is to keep smiling through,
Finding so close at hand
    The inner strength that's you.

All very well for others to preach
They really haven't a clue,
They should try swapping places
    And standing in your shoes.

Fair, fat and forty
Here's to all in this club,
Just look in the mirror
    And stroll to the pub!

The Nurse

Caring for her patients
Should be her only aim,
Using the drugs wisely
    To help ease their pain.

Demands are long and arduous
Time off very short.
Cleaning up messes
    Makes very little sport.

Her valued contributions
To her patients' welfare,
Showing her vocation
    By the way she cares.

She is needed night and day
To stretch the duty roster,
And would be sorely missed
If they ever lost her.

She should be rewarded
In many different ways,
Like provision of a carer
    When she ends her days.

Not all our nurses are women
Some of them are male,
The same dedicated spirit
    Should always prevail.

Stocktaking

How many of them in there?
How many of these bits?
It nearly drives you mad
    Sends the storeman into fits.

Last year there was twenty-three
Now, only twenty-two,
We really are in a mess
    Just don't know what to do.

Of course, some could be sold
Some, were used as spares,
Some were written off
    By the boss man up the stairs.

Roll on the end of this task
Roll on the close of today,
Oh no! we now have overtime
    And late we have to stay.

Phew! that's it for this year
Now a twelve-month break,
Now the auditors tell us
    They've found some damned mistakes.

Problems

Some problems go on and on
    Never seeming to end,
Problem shared, problem halved,
So why worry a friend?

To tackle a problem head-on
    Takes an awful lot of guts,
Sometimes it is the only way
To climb out of the rut.

Worry, heartache, stress
    All link together,
Then it seems you are
At the end of your tether.

We all get our problems
    Whatever the kind,
How we fervently wish
We could leave them behind!

Life is a problem
    Right from day one,
And will continue so
Until our life is done.

Better or Worse

Part of the marriage service
Is for better or worse,
Nobody can tell you
    Which part of it came first.

Life, is full of surprises
Like for better or worse,
It can be a blessing
    Or it can be a curse.

There's rude health or illness
Activity or converse,
Wheelchair or Roller
    Chauffeur or a nurse.

Look on the bright side
Indulge in song or verse,
Long walks in the country
    Could your health imburse.

Living today can be hard
Whatever your purse,
The struggle must go on
    Be it better or worse!

Cold, Icy Grip

The icy grip of winter
Dominates the land,
There is no escape from
    The bitter cold at hand.

The earth like cast iron
Water frozen into ice,
Many little creatures
    Will pay a deadly price.

Now the intense cold
Followed by deep snows,
Brings the transport system
    To a crawling speed so slow.

We try to carry on
In spite of winter's grip,
We see the obvious dangers
    Of a fall or slip.

Bitter cold, holds the land
And the chilling winds do blow,
How we all do yearn
    For winter's grip to go.

Avalon

Long has King Arthur been dead
But whither has he gone?
His body rests entombed
    On the Isle of Avalon.

'Tis said when England needs him
This king will rise again,
That time has surely come
    Other leaders are so lame.

We need a strong fighting king
To put our country first,
Others give too much away
    Now we fear the worse.

Europe rules our island state
We toady to the Hun,
Dig in our heels, say No!
    Creeping days are done!

King Arthur, rise from Avalon
You are needed now!
Unite our island nations and
    Fulfil your ancient vow!

Fear

Looking at life's rich pattern
And the changes year by year,
Lurking in the shadows
    Is the ghastly enemy, fear.

Whatever we choose to do
Whichever way we steer,
We are always haunted
    By the spectre hiding near.

Decisions in life, hard to make
Bring smiles or often a tear,
No need to bite your nails
    If your conscience be clear.

We are all vulnerable
However we are reared,
Difficult to separate
    Our hopes from our fears.

The lesson we should learn
Open our ears to hear,
Is we must banish the
    Bête noire enemy of fear.

Death Traps

They floated gracefully in the sky
Amongst the applause and claps,
They were really most unsafe
    Just gigantic death traps.

It was the fuel they carried
Hydrogen, prone to fire,
When ignited in error
    The ship became a pyre.

The passengers on board
Thought the flight was ace,
When it burned so swiftly
    For them no time of grace.

Nearly all on board
The *Hindenburg* died,
There was no escape
    So many were fried.

Mighty feat of engineering
So far in advance of most,
Part of history's archives
    A truly tragic ghost.

The Spider

She squats in a corner
Lurking in the dark,
When she feels a quiver
    Then out she darts.

What is entrapped
On the silken thread?
A fly struggling
    In her web.

What falls to the trap
Caught in this fatal hell?
Not sound or sight
    But a honeyed smell.

Most fear the spider
An ancient inbred dread,
Relating to the insects
    Alive or dead.

This ugly predator
Rids the house of flies,
A service we can witness
    As each spider complies.

Little Corporal

Napoleon was a corporal
Led France into war,
He was never satisfied
    Always wanting more.

Like others before him
He bit more than he could chew,
In the fullness of time
He met his Waterloo.

He made a move on Russia
In the bitter wintertime,
His army was left frozen
In the inclement clime.

He boasted he would win
Never doubting his aim,
Styling himself as emperor
Revelling in his claim.

His grandiose plans
Became but dreams,
Leaving his famous quotation
    "Not tonight, Josephine!"

St Kilda

Way out in the Atlantic
St Kilda's towering stacks
Many intrepid explorers
    Never came back.

The islanders were starving
This island so remote,
The only means of supplies
    Was delivered by boat.

Some of the brave and fittest
Collected fulmars' eggs,
A treacherous climb resulting
    In broken arms and legs.

In the end they gave up
And all had to leave,
Transported to the mainland
    Hunger pangs relieved.

Tourists in the summer
Visit the village scene
Remains of dwelling houses
    Clearly can be seen.

Proud of their history
And the Gaelic they spoke,
Which told of the hardships
    Of the island folk.

Both Leader and Led

Inside many of us
Rages a turbulent battle,
Like a petulant child
    Throws away his rattle.

Lack of control and discipline
Brings this state about,
There's usually no need
    To rave and shout.

We find we're losing ground
In the age-old battle,
We are manipulated
    Herded just like cattle.

A strong leader is required
Without tittle-tattle,
An intelligent example
    Of knowledge, not prattle.

To lead us to prosperity
Cages must be rattled,
Show some fighting spirit
    We will not be shackled.

Craving

Yearning for a substance
    Soon becomes a crave,
This abusing leads
To an early grave.

The standard treatment
    Cold turkey set,
With quakes and tremors
Nasty cold sweats.

Users of these drugs
    Stole, habit to feed,
Victims of the pushers
Who white did bleed.

Evil peddlers on the streets
    Encouraged the cravings,
Were not interested
Lives to be saving.

They pushed the substances
    Enjoying the scene,
Yet unaware
They had been seen.

So were sent to jail
    Maybe for years,
Such time in prison
Removes all careers.

When cravings are felt
    Do not turn to drugs,
For prison or graveyard
Is for idiots and mugs.

A Gaelic Song

A Highland lass was singing
Inside her crofter home,
The rich and vibrant melody
    Was absorbed in the stone.

The haunting song she sang
Refused to go away,
Hanging in the air
    It was there to stay.

She sang of crofter tales
Of their lives and loves,
Trying to raise family
    Amongst hawks and doves.

The doves bring prosperity
The hawks bring woe,
Crofters were uprooted
    And forced to go.

If you listen carefully
You can hear a Gaelic song,
Wistfully upon the air
    Where once a voice belonged.

Universal Fusion

Blazing across the heavens
Beating on the ground,
'Til all the greenery
Was shrivelled and brown.

There was no escape
For wood, lake or field,
Only mighty rocks
Provided a stony shield.

Devouring the planets
Earth was on the list,
How we fervently prayed
We could be missed.

All the living creatures
Began to die away,
As the sun expanded
Bigger each day.

Such terrible devastation
Such planetary strife,
The earth herself devoured
By the star that gave her life.

Traveller's Joy

Better known as old man's beard
This clinging traveller's joy,
Climber of the hedgerow
    Other life destroys.

A delicate looking plant
White flowering lace,
Fast growing to the top
    From tough wiry base.

Many a walker on the road
Passed by this lovely sight,
Looking for a sheltered spot
    Where to spend the night.

White, old man's beard and
This traveller's joy,
Full decorates the hedges
    Nature's flowering ploy.

Jack of All Trades

It's said a little knowledge
    Can be a dangerous thing,
Decisions without wisdom
    Disasters soon can bring.

Our Jack of all trades
    Knew a little about a lot,
Bits of gathered lore
    Thrown into the pot.

Stirred up well in the mix
    Useful when required,
His assorted information
    Many a task inspired.

He appeared to be unfulfilled
    In spite of years of fun,
Scraps of data incomplete
    Left him master of none.

This wistful poignant saga
    Leaves me rather sad,
Jack tried to do his best
    But in mind, he was only a lad.